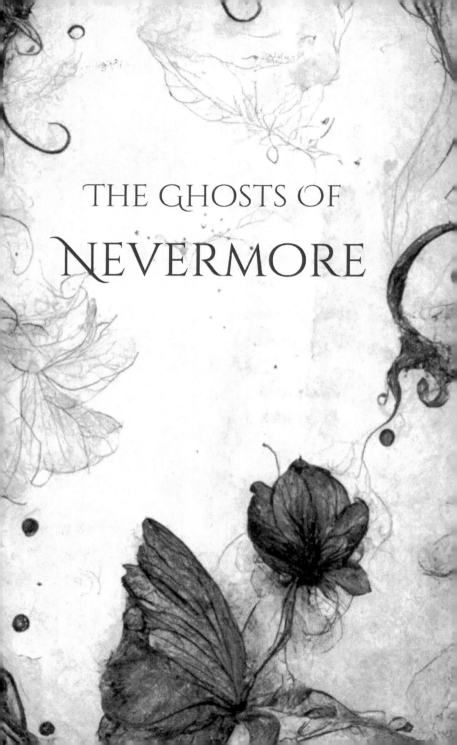

THE GHOSTS OF
NEVERMORE

Praise for the Ghosts of Nevermore

"The Ghosts of Nevermore is a breathtaking, haunting, and visually stunning collection of dark and lovely things. From the moment I opened the book, I was captivated by Trisha's artwork and Poe-inspired poetry and prose. This book will grip your heart, penetrate your soul, and stir the ghosts within."

Kristin Kory
Author-Hungry for Ghosts

"Ghosts of Nevermore is evocative, creative, and decidedly beautiful. Trisha weaves her words into the marrow of your bones and will leave you breathless, and begging for more. I definitely recommend giving this a read, then reading it again, and then passing it on."

Mira Hadlow
Author-As Muses Burn & Red

"The twists and turns will leave a bite mark on your soul."

S.A. Quinox
Author-Immortalis & Tales of Lacrimosa

THE GHOSTS OF
NEVERMORE

BY
TRISHA LEIGH
SHUFELT

POETRY, PROSE, & STORIES INSPIRED BY

EDGAR ALLAN POE

Ah, distinctly I remember

it was the bleak December;

And each separate dying ember

wrought its ghost upon the floor.

The Raven 1845

Edgar Allan Poe

To my beloved Edgar
and all the Ghosts of Nevermore.

FOREWORD

Trisha brims with depth. Her ink is not from this time and place. Her writing style takes you back to days of old and sorrow-a gothic setting where darker skies roam, and the air is an eternal mist. Cold settles in our bones, and gloom becomes our mantle. No sun dares cast its light here, for the moon is ever-present. The scene is never-ending winter, brought to us by a carriage from the ghosts of Nevermore.

But rest assured, the fireplace will be your sanctuary. Because despite this melancholy setting, Trisha will not leave you freezing. She will undoubtedly astonish you from start to finish. Edgar Allan Poe may deeply inspire her ink, but her portrayal is unique and deliciously dark.

Sit with each poem, as it will freefall into the deepest part of your heart. It will nestle there softly, like a hunger or a craving for more. If melancholy has not soothed you before, I promise you it will now.

S.A. Quinox

Author of Immortalis & Tales of Lacrimosa

Author's Note

I owe much to Edgar Allan Poe. In many respects, he saved my life. Although he's been dead for over 200 years, he is alive and well in the hearts of the legions of fans familiar with his macabre poems and stories. He's undoubtedly alive in my heart.

Like many, Edgar Allan Poe came into my life in elementary school. I remember sitting in a circle while each one of my classmates took turns reading his epic poem, the Raven. Although I understood little about the poem or author, I was utterly enthralled by its haunting imagery and musicality. Over the years, I have read my fair share of Mr. Poe's works. He's become a touchstone for inspiration in my artwork, poems, and dark fantasy novels.

When the Covid pandemic hit, I was busy finishing a Tarot deck called the Poe Tarot, which follows Edgar Allan Poe as the main character navigating the Fool's journey. It was years in the making and painfully researched. Since its launch in December 2021 to stellar reviews, it has sold worldwide, received a COVR (Coalition of Visionary Resources) Visionary Award, was nominated for a Saturday Visiter Award through

Poe Baltimore, and a CARTA Award through the International Tarot Foundation. But enough tooting my horn, back to why Poe saved my life.

In 2015, I battled breast cancer. Like many who travel this road, my life changed in more ways than one. The list is long, and I won't bore you with the details, but in a nutshell, I understood the phrase, life is short. Before 2015, I'd spent most of my life waiting for things to happen. I shank from possibility due to fear of the unknown and questioned my abilities as a writer and artist. Therefore, I shelved many projects and internalized years of doubt.

When the idea for the Poe Tarot came along, I was mentally and emotionally exhausted. However, something magical happened while researching his life and works. I found myself. I felt like he was speaking to me through my art and helping me cope with the myriad of emotions I hadn't faced until that moment. The lockdown gave me more than ample time to go within and explore. So, I did that with Poe and continue to do so to this day.

The Ghosts of Nevermore is my latest but assuredly not my last Poe-inspired endeavor. Poetry has always helped me through the shadows of this life. Who better understood the darkness within than the master of the macabre?

The ghosts of his poems and stories haunt these pages. I hope you will find comfort as I have in their presence.

Trisha Leigh Shufelt

SECTIONS

LOVE & LOSS

MADNESS & LONGING

SPIRITS & DEMONS

THE OTHERS
(DARK POETRY & PROSE WITH EDGAR IN MIND)

BEHIND THE GHOSTS

POETRY & SHORT STORIES BY EDGAR ALLAN POE
USED FOR THE GHOST OF NEVERMORE

Masque of the Red Death

Annabel Lee

Tamerlane

To One in Paradise

Eulalie

The Black Cat

A Dream

The Bells

The Lake

Evening Star

Fairy-Land

Spirits of the Dead

The Tell-Tale Heart

Murders in the Rue Morgue

Valley of Unrest

City in the Sea

The Raven

Love & Loss

"BUT THE VOID WITHIN MY
HEART REFUSED, EVEN THUS,
TO BE FILLED."

ELEONORA 1842

BELOVED

God, help my poor soul. How I long to join you in death's eternal slumber. To hold your angelic hand and kiss your crimson lips once more. How many times have I written epitaphs of love in your name only to find them sodden with grief? Melancholy memories replete with madness pump sweet horror from my broken heart. I long to turn this living blood into inky vines that pull me beneath the caliginous earth to lie forever by your side.

"God, help my poor soul."

Thought to be E.A. Poe's last words.

DEAREST

Ribbons of moonlight
curtain tenebrous twilight
with memories of an evanescent sea
and youthful places,
time endeavors to erase for us
but never my love for thee.

For as the moon ever beams
and brings me sweet dreams
of our shoreline walks together,
the angels above
who envied our love,
chilled our stolen kisses forever.

But neither last bated breath
nor my sepulcher in death
will dissever my soul from the soul of thee.
I am forever your bride
in eternities night-tide
your beloved, Annabel Lee.

Inspired by Annabel Lee 1849

ADA

If I had only loved you as I loved myself.
If I had only valued you as I did my wealth.

Regret has fall'st into my soul like rain
and marks my achievements as a bitter stain.

The pedestal I carved with ego in mind
should have been yours to sit for all time.

Yet now, in the desperate minutes, all is for
naught, for love, it seems, can never be bought.

And time has stripped me bare in my shame
as I go to my grave with only my name.

If I had one wish, I'd gladly replace
all I have for love's look on your face.

Inspired by Tamerlane 1827

ETERNAL

In the stillness that remains,
I have wept in silent pain.
But I cannot shut my eyes,
for your loss has left me blind.

And the darkness that fills my mind
still remains.

All that once was has left this home,
and nothing more shall ever grow
without you.

Without you, I am forever cold.
Nothing more shall warm these bones
till the promises we made grow old.

I'll remain
without you.

Inspired by To One in Paradise 1843

IN YOUR EYES

I remember when
what came before did stop,
and life did begin again
in your eyes.

When all that was splintered
lost its matter,
love carried it away
with the bruised and battered.
All with the violet gaze
from your eyes.

Any sorrow I thought I'd find
turned back the hands of time,
and I remember why
it all stood still for me
in the violet gaze of your eyes.

Inspired by Eulalie 1845

MEMENTO MORI

Like I, the ticking Clock laments the death of my beloved wife. A reminder that while its heart beats, she is as silent as the grave. I've longed to rid myself of the ubiquitous specter, yet find its presence a strange comfort to her memory. You see, while I was never fond of it, my angel fell under its spell the moment we moved into the renovated church, now a sprawling manor home. It had seen its fair share of births and deaths, but unlike the ghosts who had abandoned it, the stained-glass windows and the Clock were fixtures that remained.

She adored it, not the home but the Clock. Nay, I dare say she loved the Clock, perhaps even more than me. Often, upon the hour's strike, I witnessed her sway to and fro while singing a melancholy tune. When I asked to whom she sang, she always replied, 'to the dead.' I dismissed her response. She was often whimsical, even in her melancholy. I can almost hear her voice now, as though she were beckoning me to awaken from my mournful gloom. Of course, she would not wish my perpetual grief nor my spiral descent into drink and laudanum.

That is why I had to move the Clock to the undercroft at the western end of our home. You see, the Clock, like my guilt, had become an albatross. The mere sight of it brought me such torment that I could no longer bear to gaze hopelessly upon it without thinking of my beloved.

Its ebony wood, like the color of her hair.
Its curves, like the swell of her hips.
Its porcelain face, like that of
her sweet youthful skin.
Its delicate accent roses, like the
blood on her lips.

I long for absolution. I long to break free from the throes of my madness and awaken from this inconsolable grief. I long to dance with her one more time.

The bitter truth coats my tongue a reddish-brown, and I swallow my penance for the sins I must have committed to having her life deprived of mine. I distract, nay, I wallow in the mind-numbing liquid, grateful for peace, giddy in my delirium until I hear the Clock strike. The sound brings death's pallor to my face and silences my revelry.

The Clock! How could I be so selfish? I have all the luxuries in the world, a spacious and beautiful home, vices to soothe my aching soul, and the warmth of a roaring fire, but my love-she languishes in the dark with ghosts.

The Clock strikes, and my attention draws toward the moonlight streaming through the stained-glass window, infusing the room with a blue hue-my beloved's favorite color. I rise from my eastern chair to gaze upon the grounds, still fresh with spring flowers. I smile at the prospect of a new life.

Yet my attention shifts with another Clock strike, and I see the undercroft window, lit red with ambient light. A shadowy figure stares back at me, sending ice through my veins. I am a frozen corpse until I hear another strike of the Clock.

The horror! A thief in the night! I stumble at the sound, reminiscent of a woman's cry. It grows louder as I make my way through the maze of rooms, leading me toward the undercroft.

The next room illuminates with the following moon igniting a purple glow. I hesitate, unsure of my path but hear the Clock strike again, louder this time as though she were in pain. I continue to the next room, now green, and within it, I see a swirling sea of masked revelers.

The Clock strikes! They smile and nod at me in their grandeur. For a moment, I question their presence as though they were the remnants of a retreating dream. Then the sea parts, and as it does, the Clock strikes again. No longer revelers but an unholy choir singing a melody familiar to my ears. They point me toward my final destination.

Clock strike! My silent heart beats with abandon as I race through the remaining rooms.

Clock strike!
Orange.
Clock strike!
White.
Clock strike!
Violet.

I stand in front of the closed, undercroft door and see a glow, beating red like a heartbeat beneath its threshold, as red as the blood of life.

The door creaks open.

I am no longer afraid of what lies betwixt and between this life and the other. I know what awaits me on the other side. Without hesitation, I cross the threshold, and as I do, the ebony clock strikes one final time.

Her melodic voice. The sweet song to the dead falls silent within my ears. Porcelain turns sanguine, and my angel in death greets me with a welcoming kiss.

Inspired by the Masque of the Red Death- 1842

Madness & Longing

"AND HAVE I NOT TOLD
THAT WHAT YOU MISTAKE
FOR MADNESS IS BUT OVER-
ACUTENESS OF THE SENSES?

THE TELL-TALE HEART 1843

DISQUIET

Inspired by The Bells 1848

All is well,
and then I feel a tingling swell —
in the distance, a pinprick prickling
as though tiny bells are ring, ring, ringing.

Under my skin,
or perhaps, in the catacombs of my mind,
the deepest recesses remain captive to its chime,
calling me back to the rhyme
of madness long forgotten.

That chime —
that no longer distant chime
is like a living vine wrapping my spine
with the ghostly fingers of yesteryear.

And now, the chime echoes —
a tenebrous, monotonous, droning echo
breaches the surface of its grave
like the rippling rush of a clamoring,
cantankerous train —

a train roiling over my brain —
a train I can no longer contain,
howling through my veins,
tolling in its whistling wail,
the scream I can no longer curtail.

LADY OF THE LAKE

I'm captivated by the comfort of my melancholy
as she draws me ever nearer to self-desolation.

When all else has abandoned my senses, she is
quick to pinprick my heart with her torment, an
ache that is as intoxicating as it is torturous.

I say she because, like a muse that is ever present
but just out of reach, I long to give myself over to
her bittersweet depths and drown in her
poisonous bliss.

Inspired by The Lake 1827

THE REALM

Between ancient oaks
and transient mushroom blooms
lies a path where time stands still
An ancient realm
betwixt twilight and moon
where mortals dare not dwell

I'd heard the tales
but failed to yield
to the glossing woodland shadows
and stumbled upon
the veil one night
on a walk of solemn sorrows

An ancient rite
drenched in firelight
rooted me to the now
while harpist strings
and fluttering wings
broke the trance upon my brow

I felt a pull
into their tapestry
and came to rest
beneath the ground,
no longer on my woodland walk

but deep within a fairy mound

No earthy delight
could compare to the sight
of their hallowed hamlets and halls
All pleasure and sin
are free within
the drapery of their hidden walls

And should you partake
of their wine and cake,
be aware of the madness it brings
One is never satiated
at the table of the baited
nor ready for the drop of their wings

For glamour's beauty fades,
and all molders to shades
of blackened death before thine eyes
I shall never tread again
upon their moonlit woodland glen
for fear I will meet my demise

Inspired by Fairy-Land 1845-1848

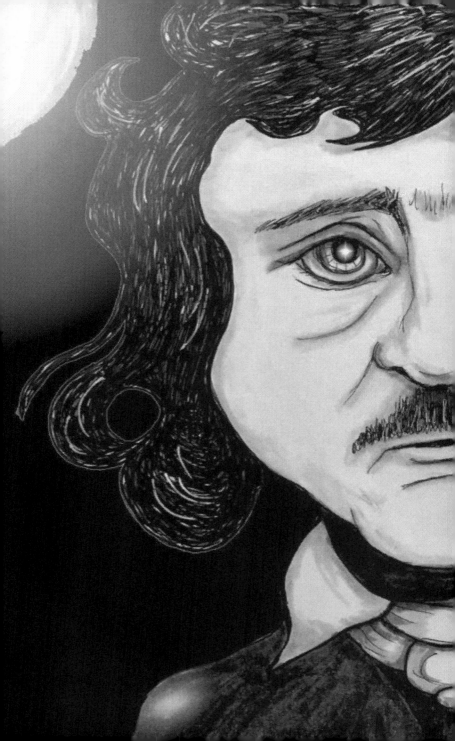

MY STAR

as I sit with thoughts that gather in gloom
beneath the weight of the mid-summer moon
the night tide surrounds me like a glove
I see a beauteous star in the distance above

she winks at me in her curious way
an affront to the moon who demands my sway
with her portentous watch as cold as her beam
my gaze shifts away toward the star's subtle
gleam

for small, she may be in her heavenly home
she shines ever brighter to my gathering gloam
and lifts my spirits as high as a dove
to warm my heart with her hope and love

Inspired by Evening Star 1827

FAMILIAR

I shall tell you a story wrapped in liquid sorrow and perpetual grief — a tale so black that it haunts my waking dreams. When I was a child of ten, a black cat crossed my path on my way home from school. Superstitions of black cats disguised as witches were commonplace, but I gave it little thought and adopted him as my own.

I was a lonely child with a mild deformity of the right eye, causing it to drift off center. Because of this, I was the target of bullies and prone to insecurities. I found it challenging to make friends and thought a pet would bring me out of my melancholy. The cat became my constant companion and confidant. With him by my side, I thought I could do anything. I named him Pluto because it is the planet farthest from the sun, which is how much I loved him.

We did everything together, and he followed me everywhere until my eighteenth year when I met a young girl named Jeza. She was a beauty who captured my heart and reminded me of my beloved cat with her sea-glass green eyes and thick black hair. Pluto did not share my fondness. Despite her attempts to woo the creature, he would hiss and growl in her presence, which she found rude. Jealous of my time with Jeza, he began to avoid me. When she would leave, he would hide under my bed for hours and even avoid his meals.

"You are punishing yourself, you insolent beast," I would say. My angry words only made him distance himself further from me.

This behavior continued until the day I asked Jeza for her hand in marriage. In my nervous state, I imbibed beforehand. When I proposed, he surprised us with his presence and appeared loving toward her. We were both hopeful about his change of heart. However, when Jeza caressed him, the beast turned and attacked her, drawing blood. Well, you can imagine my shock and horror. In a rage, I grabbed him by the nape of the neck and threw him across the room. Pluto hit the far wall with a resounding thud. My sweetheart, whom I was sure would forgive my outburst, did not. Instead, her once delicate features now twisted into an admonishing look of betrayal—something I couldn't understand. When I reached toward her, she recoiled and called me Jekyll and Hyde. Furthermore, she vowed never to see me again. I was guilt-ridden and heartbroken.

Afterward, I sought my cat, who had fled from our sight after a moment of dazed confusion. I would find him hiding under my bed. As you can imagine, he was quite shaken and, even worse, had suffered a ruptured eye from the force of the blow. Still, despite my ill-treatment, Pluto found it in his heart to forgive me.

From that moment forward, I vowed to remain loyal to him. I even convinced myself he saw something in Jeza that I could not—an evil, perhaps. In his catlike way, he was warning me that our courtship was doomed and a more suitable partner needed his approval. Pluto was more than a pet. He was my other half, and I would treat his preferences with more respect.

Still, I was a man of marrying age. My father, in particular, was eager for me to carry on the family name. Therefore, I wasted little time searching for a suitable mate. However, try as I may, I found the prospect difficult, and I began imbibing to boost my courage. This boost worked until I would bring the ladies to my home to meet Pluto. Their reaction to him determined the relationship's progression, which often ended that evening. I couldn't fault Pluto. For his part, he'd learned his lesson with Jeza and made every effort towards affection, even being overly affectionate on his first meeting. It was their blatant rejection of him that set my teeth on edge. Perhaps it was his eye that turned their fickle stomachs. Either way, I found my patience wearing thin, and as my resentment increased, so did my intake of alcohol. This was not my fault. I can assure you that I was a complete gentleman towards these women whose demeanors became frigid and cruel when shown even the slightest love and affection from Pluto.

My last attempt with a woman named Victoria is what has brought me to the woeful state you see before you now. I thought she was the one — a woman of exquisite beauty and refinement. Therefore, I became a paragon of sobriety as she found the imbibing of liquor distasteful. However, when it came time for her to meet Pluto, I was nervous, fearing she would reject him like all the others. Because of this, I allowed a few shots of whisky to allay my insecurities.

At first, all seemed well. Victoria appeared unphased by Pluto's appearance. She even welcomed him with open arms. However, as his affections increased, she rejected him, even slapping and pushing him off her like he was a demon-possessed. This enraged me. I don't know what came over me, but I struck her with a violent blow, which caused her to fall and hit her head. Victoria lay lifeless in a pool of blood, and Pluto, my beloved cat, had disappeared.

I would confess in the morning. In the meantime, I wanted to forget my guilt and the bloody deed. That night, I drank myself to excess and fell asleep on the couch, failing to extinguish a nearby candle. I awoke to the sound of Pluto's cries and the smell of smoke. I ran from the home just before it burned to the ground. In the aftermath, not even the evidence of Victoria's body remained. Perhaps, Pluto had knocked over the candle. There was no way of knowing. The only thing I knew was that he had saved me. He had also vanished again. This time, I feared the worst.

I had nowhere to go but back to my parent's home and hoped Pluto would find me. When news of the fire broke, an investigation followed. An eyewitness claimed she'd seen me with a woman who resembled Victoria. Another claimed she heard screaming coming from my house and then silence. I maintained my innocence. Besides, my reputation spoke for itself. I was an upstanding gentleman. Neither myself nor my family had ever suffered a stain on our name. In time, the whispers would disappear, or so I thought until a woman offered damning information against me.

The woman was my first love, Jeza. She claimed abuse at my hand and that my love of drink caused my Jekyll and Hyde persona. She attested that Pluto was a figment of my imagination—a device in which to seduce women. She claimed Pluto was my alter ego and a shadow side of myself that emerged upon rejection of physical advances. She mentioned the other women I'd seen who had disappeared. Despite my protests to the contrary, the police took her side and searched my property with cadaver dogs. It was an entirely unnecessary and vile affair. That was until the dogs began to dig. They unearthed the bodies of four decayed women and charged me with their murders.

Only now, in my forced sobriety, can I say that Jeza's words were not entirely false. Pluto was indeed a part of me. The side that loved me more than anyone had ever loved me, and he was as real as I am sitting before you today. He was my awakened self and my self-desolation. However, as loyal as he was, he could not save me from my demons or my spiral descent into hell.

Inspired by the Black Cat 1843

IN BETWEEN

Somewhere between dreams and reality resides bittersweet Hope. A bearable illusion while dreaming, yet unattainable in the painful truth of my wakefulness.

In my conscious reflection, I regret the times Hope touched me unaware and now appears as a distant dream.

I pray for sleep that takes me to the place between so I may remain in blissful delusion for all eternity.

Inspired by *A Dream 1827*

Spirits & Demons

"BELIEVE NOTHING YOU HEAR, AND ONLY ONE HALF THAT YOU SEE."

THE SYSTEM OF DR. TARR AND PROFESSOR FETHER 1845

A Bird's Tale

I believe in ghosts, not the kind in white sheets that rattle chains, but the ones that haunt memories and leave energetic imprints in houses and on battlefields. Some things you can't unsee, as though your eyes take a forever picture and hang it on the walls of your mind. You can try to cover the image, but it's still there, like a scar after a deep cut.

That's how it was for me. I didn't know much about him, but I will never forget his eye. I say eye because one differed from the other, and the imprint burned in my brain still haunts me today. Just as the writer must write, every heart has a tale to tell, even those that cease to beat.

I'm comfortable with death. I've been around it my entire life. My parents are morticians whose business is in an old Victorian home. Growing up, I'd seen my fair share of dead bodies and oddities. Nothing phases me, and they taught me early on not to fear death. As far as I am concerned, death is as natural as life, and my parent's volition is a job, plain and simple. Even the smell of formaldehyde is calming to me.

My mother named me Rue after the herb Ruta graveolens that Ophelia gives to Hamlet's mother for her hasty marriage to Hamlet's Uncle following his father's untimely death. Many believe it is a symbol of regret and repentance. I always wondered if it held meaning for my mother but never asked. Unlike my father, she was often distant and unapproachable.

My father started my death journey by teaching me insect taxidermy. He equated the embalming process to prepping entomological specimens and suturing dead flesh to pinning insects. Of course, all of my father's clientele were human and already dead, but he thought killing live insects using cotton wool dipped in acetone and a glass jar would ease my discomfort in handling dead bodies. I'll admit that I struggled with the cruelty of this process, but in time the insect's transition from life to death intrigued me.

After graduating from insects, I learned to prep human bodies for embalming. Oddly enough, when it came time to work with my first dead human, I did so with ease. While most teenagers were busy dating and attending parties, I washed and massaged the dead. Nudity has never been an issue for me. I simply viewed it as another layer of clothing.

Still, it's a lonely job, and I often create stories about the deceased — stories I think they would like better than the lives they lived. For example, Joe Carmino, age 62, who worked as a plumber and died of cardiac arrest, was now Josephani 'the Squid' Blackwood, who made his living as a pirate, pilfering rare coins off the coast of Madagascar. I don't know if such an occupation exists, but it sounds good.

One evening while my parents were out celebrating their wedding anniversary and I was home relaxing with some herbal tea and reruns of I Love Lucy, the doorbell rang. I figured it was the pizza I'd ordered; however, no one was there when I opened the door. Who was I kidding? It was probably some local kids playing doorbell dash with the creepy funeral home again. These childish pranks always happened as we got closer to Halloween. Besides, the stoner pizza delivery dude was never on time. It would be a good hour before I saw my cold veggie supreme. As I was shutting the door, an autumn breeze blew past me, chilling me to the bone. I grabbed my tea and a sweater and went downstairs to organize the supplies in the mortuary. I'd promised my parents I'd get this done while they were out. Hell, I'd probably finish before my pizza even arrived.

Upon entering, I saw a body on my work table. Father hadn't mentioned any new customers. I laughed to myself. I always called them customers. Perhaps it had slipped his mind, given the anniversary celebrations. I blew out my lips, grabbed the intake sheet, and pulled back the covering on the body. It was an elderly gentleman dressed in a long pinstriped dressing gown.

William Bird
Age 82
Death-Heart failure

"Okay, William, let's get you cleaned up," I said, removing his clothing. No next of kin to return personal belongings was noted, so I threw his gown in the incinerator. Then I washed him with a microbial disinfectant and massaged his limbs to prevent rigor mortis. Father had begun letting me set the facial features by suturing the lips and using a unique eye cap to set the eyes. This is where my insect pinning experience came in handy. As it was my way to pass the time, I colored over his intake information with something more fantastical.

I stared at his face for several minutes. Most of the deceased I handled looked peaceful in their eternal repose. However, something in his features suggested betrayal. I couldn't put my finger on it, but I could see it embedded in the lines on his forehead.

"You have a good name, William. I'll leave that alone. But someone hurt you, didn't they? Someone you trusted? That's a shame. Oh well, the dead tell no tales," I said, turning to grab my tools.

Then I heard a sound, almost like an exhale of air, and caught the scent of cadaverine and putrescine, a rotting fish scent that happens with body decomposition.

"You are ripe, my friend. Father will need to pump you up right away." Everything looked normal, and I turned away again, imagining his story as I gathered my tools.

"Perhaps, you were a blacksmith or a writer. Yes. That's it. You wrote historical romance novels about famous tyrants and their lovers," I said with a slight giggle.

"That's not my story."

I dropped my tools to the floor with a resounding clang and turned to see William Bird sitting upright.

"Fucking rigor mortis, and I am hearing things!" I'd never been spooked by the dead and wasn't going to have an issue with them now. I took a deep breath, picked up the fallen tools, and placed them on a tray. Then I walked over to William Bird to lay him back on the table. As I started to position him, his right eye opened. Startled, I fell back against the tray table, knocking several glass jars to the ground. Two shattered, while a third rolled across the floor and came to rest in front of an old metal cabinet.

Silence engulfed everything, including my breath. All I could hear was my heartbeat in my ears as the corpse of William Bird stared at me with his vulture-like eye covered in blue film.

I grabbed a nearby scalpel and pointed it at him. "Wh—what the hell?" I stammered.

"Hell is right," he said from his reanimated mouth. His vulture eye blinked once while the other remained shut.

"You're dead," I said, trying to steady my shaking hand.

"That I am," the corpse replied. "But I am not finished. I *have been* betrayed."

I looked around as though someone was in the room with me, witnessing the phenomenon. We were alone. Even my phone, which would have been a convenient tool to record the event, was nowhere in sight.

"Do not fear me, Rue. I mean you no harm," he said.

"How do you know my name?"

"The dead know everything," he replied.

"What do you want from me?"

William Bird's head cocked twice to the right like a mechanical doll. "Help."

I looked toward the door, calculating how fast it would take me to reach it. "Help you with what?" I asked.

"Rrrrrrrevenge," he growled.

🜄

"I can't believe I'm doing this," I mumbled, opening the door to the passenger side of my father's hearse. William Bird's corpse, now dressed in my mother's pink floral bathrobe, plunked into the seat and sat back against the leather cushions. All I could think of was the movie, Weekend at Bernie's.

"It's not like you're going to die by going through the windshield, but everyone wears a seatbelt when I'm driving," I said, buckling him in. Once settled, I shut the door and got behind the wheel.

"Where are we going?"

"247 Hydemore Lane," he replied.

I punched the address into the GPS, put the car in drive, and took one last look in the rearview mirror. I'd lost all my appetite and imagined the delivery dude would be pretty pissed when he finally delivered my pizza and found no one home.

As we made our way along the winding roads, I caught a glimpse of his face, or should I say his eye, out of the corner of mine. The bulging blue marble stared straight ahead. Every few seconds, it would blink, accompanied by a mouth twitch. Before I decided to drive him to exact his revenge, he'd explained that his caretaker, Henri, had murdered him to steal his fortune. When I mentioned his files indicated no signs of foul play, nor did I discover anything contrary on his body, he said, 'you fancy me mad.'

I laughed. I thought the whole thing was mad. After all, I was talking to a dead guy. I couldn't imagine how I would explain this to my parents. As far as they and I, until now, were concerned, corpses did not come back to life, and ghosts did not exist. The dead were dead, and that was the end of their story. So, either I was crazy, or William Bird was more than a walking corpse; he was a ghost with a mission. I hoped that in helping him, I hadn't become an accessory to a murder revenge machination.

"This is it," William Bird said as we neared a long driveway.

I stopped the car before the entrance to a towering manor home reminiscent of all the haunted houses from my childhood dreams.

"Hey, I know this house." Everyone in town knew *this* house. "You're a famous writer or *were* a famous writer. You wrote mystery novels or something?"

"Gothic horror," he said, staring out the window with his large blue marble eye that seemed to be growing bigger by the moment.

I nodded, feeling my stomach lurch. "Look, I've brought you this far. I think it's best if we part ways. You go do your revenge thing, and when you're done, come back to my house so we can put you to rest."

That's when William Bird turned to face me. His bulging eye twitched and from it fell a pearlescent tear. I sighed at his sudden humanness, his aliveness. How could I turn away and not help him? He reminded me of the living insects I watched die in jars. My heart couldn't bare his sorrow.

"Fine," I said. "But before I help you, I have one question."

William Bird nodded.

"Why me?

"You'll see," he replied and pointed to the house.

He hadn't answered my question, but as I put the car in gear, William Bird placed his icy hand on top of mine. "No. We walk from here," he said.

I wasn't enthused about how long it might take me to run back to the car should something go wrong. He was already dead, but I wasn't. Still, I agreed. I tried to get him to reveal more of his story along the road, but he refused. Once we reached the front door, I turned to him and asked if we should knock.

"That won't be necessary," he said, pushing the door open. The hinges squealed as we stepped over the threshold and into the house. Dim overhead lights cast enough glow to see, and I followed him through a series of rooms until we reached a library. A beautiful copy of Shakespeare's Hamlet sat on a desk in the center of the room.

"Was this where you wrote your stories?" I asked in a hushed tone.

He nodded and walked over to a small area rug in front of the desk. He coughed into his hand when he faced me, causing his eye to bulge. "Take this. It's for Henri," he said.

I grimaced at what he might be holding but crossed the room to find it was a deathwatch beetle. As soon as he placed it in my hand, the room illuminated.

"Who the hell are you?"

I turned to see a man standing in the doorway in his pajamas with a brass candelabra raised over his head like a weapon. His trembling hand betrayed the cadence of his demand. I looked over my shoulder to see that William Bird had disappeared. Regret filled my veins, and for a moment, all I could hear was the ticking sound of the deathwatch beetle.

I cleared my throat, trying to think of something to say that didn't sound crazy. *Yes, I'm from the local mortuary, and I followed the ghost of your former employer, who has a bone to pick with you.* "I knocked, but no one answered. I apologize for just wandering in, but I'm a big fan of your employer."

The man lowered his hand, but his expression remained baleful. "Mr. Bird is not with us, and I am not giving tours of his estate any time soon."

"I'm sorry to hear that he passed," I said, trying to remain calm.

"I never said he was dead. Now, will you kindly leave before I—" The man stopped speaking and looked around. "What's that sound?"

"I don't hear anything?" I lied.

Sweat met the man's forehead. "You must hear it. It sounds like a heartbeat." I watched him spin in a wild circle and then move closer to me.

"It's coming from you! What's that in your hand? Give it to me this instant!"

I held out my hand to reveal the deathwatch beetle. "William Bird wanted me to give this to you," I said.

All the color drained from his face, and he dropped the candelabra to the wood floor.

"That's—that's a heart," he stammered.

He was right. The deathwatch beetle was gone. In its place was a small human heart. But as it pulsed to life, it grew several sizes until it filled my hand.

"William Bird gave it to you? That's not possible," the man said. "I took care of him. I knew his every move. Who the hell are you?"

"My name is Rue. William said this was for you," I repeated, holding the beating heart out to him.

"Ruuuuuuuuuuuuuuuue," he replied, drawing out my name in a sarcastic way that made me sick to my stomach. "You're Pauline's Rue."

Pauline was my mother. I couldn't imagine how this man knew her.

"You think you can waltz in here and lay claim to his fortune!" he shouted.

"I don't know what you are talking about. How do you know my mother?"

"Your mother was William Bird's daughter! That makes you his—"

"Granddaughter," I murmured in sudden shock. I now understood why William Bird had come to me for help.

The thumping heart grew louder, and as it did, it sounded less like a heartbeat and more like a voice calling out the name Hen-ri, Hen-ri, Hen-ri. The caretaker's face contorted into several different emotions, the most predominant being fear.

"It's saying my name! He's dead! I know it!" he shouted and pushed me aside. I watched him remove the small area rug to reveal an old trap door. He then grabbed the latch and pulled it open. The smell of decay filled the air. "There! See, he's down there."

I peered inside and grimaced at the dismembered remains of my grandfather.

Just as Henri was about to lunge toward me, the ghost of William Bird rose from the hole. His bulging eye pulsed like the heart in my hand, and he fixed his gaze on his former caretaker. "Tell her what you did to me!" William Bird commanded, following Henri around the room until he had him backed up to the edge of the trap door.

Henri looked down into the pit and then back up at me. His features twisted into a maniacal sneer that turned into unhinged laughter. "I killed him! I killed the old man! I chopped him up into little pieces and buried him beneath the floorboards! It was his eye! That damn eye! Watching me all the time! Watching my every move! Watching me in my sleep! I couldn't take it anymore!"

A self-satisfied smile met William Bird's face, and as it did, Henri's twisted laughter turned into a desperate gasp for air. He reached toward the ghost of William Bird one last time before falling back into the bloody pit.

The room grew still, and the beating heart disappeared until all that remained was the deathwatch beetle's faint ticking sound. I looked at my grandfather, who looked more alive than I could have ever imagined.

"Thank you, dear Granddaughter. Thank you for helping me avenge my death. I'm sorry we never connected until now. I was and always have been a stubborn old man. I was never the best father to your mother," he said, picking up the book of Hamlet. "We had a terrible fight before you were born. I never approved of her marriage to your father and her pregnancy out of wedlock. Please do not blame her for my foolish mistakes. That is why I have left you my entire estate. Perhaps, it will be enough for her to forgive me," he said, holding the book out to me.

I opened the bookmarker to Ophelia's speech. While I now understood the origin of my name, I also felt overwhelmed by his gift.

"When my body is found, my lawyers will see that my estate goes to you. It was always going to go to you. Henri thought he could change that in the end.

I just wanted justice."

"You mean revenge," I smiled.

William Bird smiled in return. "Well, I did write horror."

We both laughed but then all grew silent, including the ticking beetle.

"I must bid you adieu," he said. With his last words, William Bird closed his vulture-like eye and disappeared from my sight.

~Eight Months Later~

"Is it straight?" my father asked, adjusting the sign above the entrance to William Bird's old manor estate that now read Rue Mortuary.

My mother and I stood beside each other, looking toward the house. "It's straight," she replied and turned to me. "I still can't believe you want to move into this place, let alone open your own mortuary."

"Maybe I'll give tours or take up horror writing like him," I replied.

My mother sighed. She was still struggling with her forgiveness. "Don't you think it's bad enough someone murdered him in his own home? He probably haunts the damn place. Well, if you do decide to give tours, I'm sure his horror fans will love it. Although, your grandfather was always such a recluse. He's probably rolling in his grave."

I looked down at the tiny jar in my hands and smiled. A silent deathwatch beetle rested on a bed of cotton wool. "Actually, I think my grandfather would approve."

Inspired by the Tell-Tale Heart
& Murders in the Rue Morgue

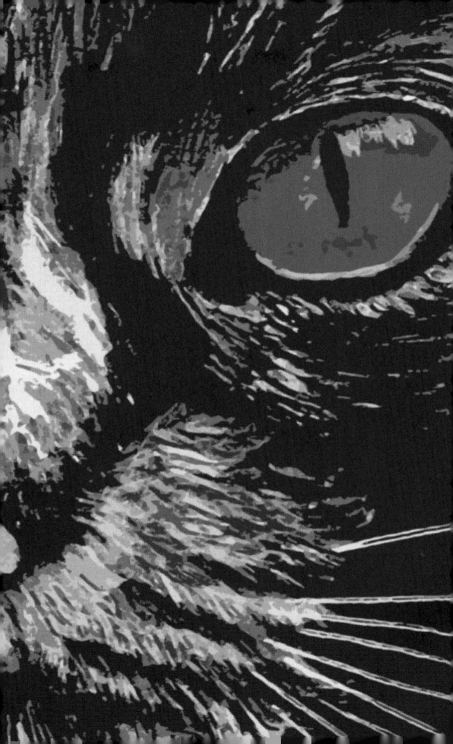

My Name Is...

Although my appearance
may fill you with fright,
I can assure you
I'm a friend of your plight.

It brings me no pleasure
to call in your hour of despair,
but the time has come to relinquish
your tether to my care.

Trust that I will hold your death
as precious as your birth
and look after those you leave
behind on this earth.

While you may feel alone
and cling to dark thoughts,
they are misplaced means of comfort-
an attempt to hold on for naught.

You, my friend, are never alone.

Unburden yourself
and place your hand and fear in mine.
Open your eyes and see
the surrounding souls who shine.

Those who have passed
as dew drops upon the grass.
They, too, were afraid
but, in the end,
traded sorrow for the spade.

They laid to rest
their troubles in mind,
assured I would keep them
all in due kind.

My name is Grief,
I'm a trusted friend,
your servant in death,
and your means to an end.

Inspired by Spirits of the Dead 1827

HAUNTED

listen to the empty house

imprints seeping through cracked plaster

ghostly voices lamenting torment from leaky
pipes

all the unsaid things

now revealed through peeling wallpaper

unhindered by age

while everything neglected remains buried

under layers of ugly paint

wood-worn floorboards sag with the weight

of what once was,

what could have been,

what still remains

backscatter memories linger like cigarette
smoke,

ancient reminders of bad choices,

insincere promises

and pain so present,

it cries remembrance in every rusty door hinge

maybe it wants to be heard

the way *we* want to be heard,

in our creaking, worn-out bones,

in our thoughts unhindered by age,

in buried regrets now quivering off our rusty
lips,

in what we can no longer contain behind our
leaky eyes

what once was,

what could have been,

what still remains

Inspired by the Valley of Unrest 1831

ASLEEP

No one saw the sparrow
or heard him over the vespering din
as he took his throne above them,
anointed by their sins.

Yet, still, they had called upon him
with their apathetic trite
and worshiped in unconscious volition
as though a sacred rite.

Harbinger of peace, they spouted
through their salty fervid tears
and built effigies in his honor
to wall their misplaced fears.

Then they went about their business,
resolute in their faction
while Death ruled above them,
masked in duplicitous satisfaction.

But lo, a stir is in the air
as salty tears turn scarlet red,
and the mouths of graves sprang open,
calling for the dead.

Not one awakened

from their complicitous slumbering sleep
as Hell greeted his flock
before rising among the sheep.

Then Death, now finished,
stepped down from his golden throne,
and Hell smiled upon him
for the reverence he had shone.

And taking his rightful seat
with an austere delight,
Hell bid Death a grateful adieu
and dismissed his evanescent flight.

Inspired by the City in the Sea 1845

THE VISITOR

My mind surrenders
in the bleak December
to the inscape of my chilling gloom.

I beg forgiveness
in the silent stillness
in which my bedlam has me entombed.

In my sorrow,
I yearn for *no* tomorrow
and pray to the harbingers of death.

They shadow my senses
with pin-pricking stasis
as needles withdraw my last dying breath.

The moonlight fades
as the curtain cascades
like her dress upon entering the room.

My eyes curtain close
in the deepest repose
as I catch the scent of death's sweet perfume.

A dreamscape awaits
through garden and gate
and at last, I see my long-lost Lenore.

Praise be the heavens above,
my angel in love,
has returned to me forevermore.

Heartbreak's embrace
drops the mask from her face
while cursed remembrances haunt her dark eyes.

Cloaked a raven, not dove,
nor from heaven above
but a Judgment upon me in disguise.

My evil sins ripen and turn sanguine,
damning me to eternity's torturous lament.

Tis, justice well served.
I nod unreserved
at my penance that lacks quiescence.

With wings, she takes flight
in the arcane crescent night.
There is nothing left of my beloved Lenore.

Still, my bedlam remains
in the construct of chains,
and the reality, she will seek me nevermore.

Inspired by the Raven 1845

The Others

"IS ALL THAT WE SEE

OR SEEM

BUT A DREAM WITHIN A

DREAM."

A DREAM WITHIN A DREAM 1849

OCTOBER GIVES BIRTH

With numb fingers and frozen toes,
October dances a dirge of death
to songs created by her crows
while winter watches with bated breath.

Variegated leaves crush beneath her feet-
chased by dusky twilight shadows.
The Queen of Faerie, she will greet
with her book of lost tomorrows.

She feeds on acorns, arsenic, and old lace,
washing it down with herbal tea
while candlelight veils her aging face,
lined with memories of what will never be.

As her reign now ushers a somber close,
she births a child with delight,
whose frost blue lips recite winter prose
of mother's wisdom to mortal's enlight.

THE PROMISES OF EVERMORE

tell me a story
about midnight
and stardust,
about daydreams
and bloodlust

feed me grapes
fermented in sin
as our fingers dance
on unrepentant skin

as dusky shadows
hang low like memory eaves,
let's reminisce the time away
on a bed of velvet leaves

for once upon a time,
not so long ago,
our thorns were lovely roses
blooming a youthful glow

time has endeavored to alter,
through the salt of winter's kiss,
the gifts that we remember
and others choose to dismiss

so let us bathe in twilight
and read love's written lore,
still ripe beneath our inky veins,
the promises of evermore

DEATH IS A COLLECTOR

I think Death is a collector,
looking upon us as works of art
to warm her walls
and as books full of melancholy poetry
to crack her heart for all eternity.

PANDORA'S BOX

I have opened it
all the beautiful, dark things,
hidden, not in a box but in a reticent portal

a rabbit's hole of pent-up poisons

a sarcophagus of candlelit rooms
and inky black thoughts

a place where I fail to breathe
but desire to live

a place where I fear I may lose my sanity
in the quest for my awakening

QUEEN OF HELL

Battle your madness with a poetic tongue.
Weave its whisperings like golden threads
through your hair.
Wear your shadow like a second skin
and forge your tears into a sacred crown.

But make no mistake,
you rule the demons of your hell
and not the other way around.

ANXIETY'S PULL

caught in the eventide of my thoughts
drowning in the resonating undertow
of my chaos
I drink in the shadows of my bitter wine

I feast on nettled fruit pies,
using ingredients purchased and grown
from shared recipes
and others of my making

until my belly aches and bloats
until thorns breach from under my nails
until a thousand saturnine seeds spew
from my bruised, teeth-bitten lips,
releasing me from this copious hell

then and only then did I empty this vessel,
and in the silence,
hear my voice
calling me to salvation

WANDERLUST

Dance me in the twilight hours
when the moon awaits her dawning,
and the sun escapes her calling.

Unwind me inch by inch
and stroke by stroke
until I leave all my broken offerings
with the hands of time.

From my barred throat,
devour my severed soul
until it is unknown and forgotten.

I want to become serene
in my wanderlust with you.

CHASING GHOSTS

your darkest desire
is a raindrop on my lips
it tastes of red wine and sweet surrender
an unquenched ache to subjugated bliss

it's a butterfly kiss on your quivering cheek
a sober thought after the diversion of drink
it's a night of salvation on the altar of the weak
that loses all meaning from the words that you
speak

And still, you chase after my ghost, who haunts
the corridors of your mind.

Nevermore

when words have lost all meaning
and shadows curtain your mind
let not your demons sway you
nor root their nest deep inside

let the waves of pain crash over you
like the sea upon the shore
let the salt peel away the layers born
and cast them out to Nevermore

the ghosts of the past need not anchor you in
their depths

I WISH FOR SILENCE

I wish for silence—
where I am undisturbed by noise pollution
and fallacious chatter

an Amity where fiery vitriolic words
extinguish to ash

a sacred place where demonic imprints
are mute in reverence, healing lamented wounds
without recompense

I wish for silence—
where love shone in the eyes needs no words yet
conveys a canvas mellifluous with meaning

where the lightest touch sings a thousand
sensations under the skin

where the quiescent chrysalis births euphonious
mysteries from the infinite universe

I wish for silence so ubiquitous
it becomes like the air I breathe,
resonating in its own unconscious vibration
heard only through the filter of my soul

SHE

Like fine leaf lines, your memory seeks a vein no longer pulsing with life and falls as pieces of death from my soul, blanketing me in quiet discontent.

I am resolute to languish in your loss, for all I have ever truly loved has been ephemeral to my heart and a ghost to my senses.

MIDNIGHT MUSES

While the living sleep,
oil lamps blaze,
illuminating willowy shadows
from their eternal rest.

The midnight muses are awake.

I hover my frozen fingers above heat vapors
as blood flows like ink to parchment,
and words follow from my mind.

My beautiful lost muses are here.

I have grieved for each of you,
hungered for your breast,
longed to say goodbye in your final rest,
and worshiped at your altar
as you took your last breath.

You invade my waking dreams
and curse my restless nights.

My soul is a sodden well
drowning in saturnine tears.

My heart is a broken compass

that seeks Memory's stolen path.

As the world trembles and turns,
I long for Death to break Time's hourglass
and scatter my dust to the forgotten winds
in a plea your ghosts haunt me nevermore.

POETS DON'T CRY

her skin laced with broken thorns
hides the tattered soul of youth
and the demons that she lies with
don't offer her their truth

she's a poet in the wasted dark
burning shadows from her roots
a strangled soul with battle scars
bleeding stories no longer mute

and she cries
from the inkwell of her mind.
yes, she cries
cuts and runs, and hides
yes, she cries
all those bitter truths and lies
until she bleeds
all those deep-rooted seeds
yes, she bleeds

the puppet masters in her head
lay waste on sacred ground
drowning her to heartbreak
over stories that kept her bound

she needles her skin in torment,
pins pricking to the sound
of lamenting souls whose warpath

thunders upon the ground

and she cries
from the inkwell of her mind
yes, she cries
cuts and runs, and hides
yes, she cries
all those bitter truths and lies
until she bleeds
all those deep-rooted seeds
yes, she bleeds

poets, don't cry, my love
they bleed words from a restless mind
and scatter all their pain and tears
like broken glass in the hands of time

until they bleed
on the paper that you read
yes, they bleed
all those deep-rooted seeds
yes, they bleed
on blood-soaked bended knees

they all bleed
until the paper tears and blows away

LOST & FOUND

I believe I was a black-winged bird in another
life with smoke for wings and silver starlight for
eyes.

My family was a murder of crows whose restless
souls fed on insatiable muses beneath hallowed
moons.

We lived in Salem, but our spirits stretched to
the Romanian shores.

Time separated us through the winds of fate
until only whispers remained of our gypsy souls.

Sometimes those whispers leave poetry from
memory's forgotten shadows as broken feathers
to seed the barren ground.

CRONE

Lost youth now feathered with fine lines
are trails of ancient wisdom birthed.

And from her silver hair glows a woven crown
of fairytales unearthed.

Her collarbone extends to thorny wings
as she takes to the ash-encrusted night.

And from her lips, the ravens sing
their songs with mirthful delight.

THE GHOSTS OF YESTERYEAR

This thing we call time. Is it our making or a dream within a dream?

Does it only exist in our imagination?

Here today and then gone the next. The present becomes the past, forever ephemeral but no more than a liminal lens to the eye of the beholder.

Everything yields to time. Even these words shall fade to whispers that surrender to remembrances carried only by the forgotten ghosts of yesteryear.

Is time, therefore, simply a cliche?

Time heals all wounds. As though pain measures less with each passing day and is no more than a thing we say when the weight of time's presence is too much of a burden to bear.

Time is of the essence, for as we know, life is short, and death is sure.

The third time is the charm, as though it were a magical spell to conjure when all else that has manifested lacks substance.

If time is an illusion, what are we, if not an illusion, in the construct of our own mind?

INKWELL

A writer's sanctuary is something only the writer understands.

For me, it's a place where the walls have teeth,

shadows are sculpted from sorrow, and perpetual winter wraps its frozen fingers around my heart.

There is comfort in this liminal space betwixt and between life and death, where delusion is a dalliance driven by Melancholy's madness.

Moonlit rain upon the window laces forgotten tears toward the inked parchment in Memory's desperate exchange.

Ghosts of Muses past linger in smoke-extinguished candle flames.

They embed their lost souls in the wax drippings, suspended in time within the woodgrain of my desk.

They are stories awaiting the pen.

The last remnants of voices longing to be heard.

Strangled imprints imprisoned by doubt and hindered by means they cannot breach.

I am their catalyst, and they are my salvation.

THE BOUNDARIES WHICH
DIVIDE LIFE FROM DEATH
ARE BEST SHADOWY AND
VAGUE. WHO SHALL SAY
WHERE ONE ENDS, AND
WHERE THE OTHER
BEGINS?

THE PREMATURE BURIAL

EDGAR ALLAN POE

BEHIND THE GHOSTS

(POEMS & STORIES USED AS INSPIRATION)

Masque of the Red Death is a short story published in 1842. It follows Prince Prospero as he tries to avoid a plague known as the Red Death by hiding in his abbey with his wealthy friends and nobles. A masquerade ensues through 7 colored rooms. All is well until the prince discovers a mysterious stranger among his guests. Once confronted, the prince finds Death comes to us all.

Annabel Lee is a haunting poem about love and loss. It was the last poem by Edgar Allan Poe and published in 1849, the same year as his death. Many speculate that Poe wrote it about his beloved wife Virginia, who died two years prior at 27. The poem's vivid description and lyrical content make it one of Poe's most recognizable poems. God help my poor soul.

Tamerlane is a poem written in 1827 that follows the life of a Turkish conqueror by the same name. Tamerlane trades the love of a peasant girl named Ada for wealth and power. It is not until his deathbed that he regrets his decisions and the loss of his beloved.

To One in Paradise is a poem about love and loss where the narrator laments over someone who was his refuge and light. He feels he will never love again and sees the world around him as dark and bleak. Only in his dreams does he find some sense of inner peace and will to continue living.

Eulalie is a poem also known as a bridal song. In it, a man overcomes his deep sadness by marrying a woman named Eulalie. Once again, Poe focuses his works on the death of a beautiful woman. Many critics feel it is autobiographical due to Poe's experience with his mother, stepmother, and wife's deaths.

The Black Cat is a short story told from the narrator's perspective, where he tells a tale that he feels no one will believe. It focuses on his relationship with a cat named Pluto, who is mutually gentle and kind. However, as things go from bad to worse for the narrator, he begins to abuse the cat and eventually sees him as a demon responsible for his misfortune.

A Dream is a poem in which the narrator speaks on feelings of hope he experiences in the dreaming state versus what he does while awake.

The Lake is a poem where Poe contrasts the dark imagery of a lake while simultaneously describing the comfort it brings him.

Evening Star is a lyrical poem in which the narrator sees all stars in the sky as cold except one bright shining star. Some feel the contrasting elements describe the unsatisfactory relationship he finds himself in and the woman he truly desires.

The Bells is a poem with musical quality that begins in merriment with the sound of sleighbells and progresses with sinister intent to a crescendo of terror that many feels signify death itself.

Fairy-Land is a poem that was initially titled Heaven. In it, Poe describes nature in all its beauty and mystery as inhabited by faeries.

Spirits of the Dead describes death as a great and beautiful mystery one should appreciate, for even if we are alone in life, in death, we will find comfort in the spirits of those who have passed.

Valley of Unrest is a poem where Poe uses imagery and metaphors to describe an imaginary landscape of life and death in war.

City in the Sea is a gothic poem about a doomed city ruled by Death that sinks into the sea.

The Raven is perhaps Poe's most well-known and beloved poem. In it, a nameless narrator laments over the loss of his beloved Lenore while a mysterious Raven causes him further torment with the repeated word, Nevermore.

The Tell-Tale Heart is a first-person narrative story about an unnamed narrator who believes himself sane but suffers from an "over-acuteness" of the senses, making him commit a horrendous crime.

Murders in the Rue Morgue-a murder mystery. Thought to be the first modern detective story.

WITH GRATITUDE

My deepest gratitude to S.A Quinox, aka Lady of the Lake for the lovely foreword. I am honored to call you, my friend.

To my talented and inspiring arc readers, Kristin Kory, Mira Hadlow, and S.A. Quinox who took on the task of reading the Ghosts of Nevermore. Your words of encouragement mean more to me than I can possibly express.

To Laura Sheridan for the use of her photography for the cover of the Ghost of Nevermore. You can find her haunting photography at laurasheridan.com

Thank you, Francesca at the Gypsy Craftery, for the beautiful ephemera images throughout the book. You can find her images at gypsycraftery.etsy.com

And finally, thank you, Edgar Allan Poe, for your continued inspiration and support of my muse.

Please visit & show your support to-poemuseum.org, poeinbaltimore.org, & eapoe.org

ABOUT THE AUTHOR

Trisha Leigh Shufelt is a self-taught artist, author, wife, mother, and cancer survivor.

Author/Artist Works Include
The Poe Tarot
The Everglow
Schiffer Publishing/RedFeatherMBS

Indie Published works include-
Liminal Lines- Poetry & Prose
Liminal Lessons- Poetry & Art
Break & Bloom- Poetry & Prose
The Ghosts of Nevermore-Poetry & Prose

Indie Published under the pen
Andaleigh Archer include-

The Underwood Wicked Fairytale Series

The Promise ~A Faerie's Tale
Red Cinder Swan
Wicked Thorns
Little Red

Coming Soon-
Brew

You can find out more about Trisha at

www.artinsoul.org

QUOTH THE RAVEN
"NEVERMORE."

THE RAVEN 1845

Made in the USA
Middletown, DE
14 October 2023